Hello, and a very big welcome to Issue 25 of [...] This month, in honour of its second birthday [...] a make-over, with a new cover style and lot[...] through - I do hope you like it!

And there's a new photograph of me too - wi[...] Bustle & Sew team - little Daisy who, at the time of writing, is just 12 weeks old. She's a proper little madam who is into everything and poor harassed Ben is trying very hard to remember exactly why he wanted a baby sister! He's very kind and patient with her though, even though she's bounced on him so much and ruffled his tummy fur into such tangles he's had to have a very short trim - a little chilly in February!

But even though the weather's still a bit chilly, here in the magazine we're looking ahead to spring, with the Daisy Knot Bag - ideal for that transition between the winter and summer seasons. You'll also find Birds on a Wire - a great way to display anything that can be pegged to a line - as well as three pretty eco-totes to keep in your handbag for those impromptu shopping expeditions!

Have a wonderful February - and I'll be back in March with some Easter ideas for you.

Helen xx

Contents:

Notes from a Devon Village	Page 4
Birds on a Wire	Page 6
Crazy Patchwork - a very Victorian Trend?	Page 9
Three Patchwork eco-Totes	Page 11
Really Easy Fabric Covered Lampshades	Page 19
Valentine's Greetings	Page 21
Owls in Love	Page 22
Made for Each Other Love Heart	Page 26
Transferring your Design	Page 30
Vintage Pattern: Moonlight Capers	Page 33
Daisy Knot Bag	Page 37
Hints & Tips from Stitchers	Page 41
Mice are Nice Embroidery	Page 42
An Alphabet of Stitches (part 4)	Page 49

Notes from a Devon Village

February, although the coldest month of the year here in England, is also the last month of winter and there is a sense of life beginning to stir beneath the frozen land.

If you look very closely there are tiny buds on the hawthorne hedges where, before too much longer, there will be fresh green leaves, the snowdrops are already in bloom and the hardy green spikes of daffodils and narcissi stand strong and proud above the bare earth.

Signs of spring indoors on my mantlepiece

I will hang my special "dog-fur station" in the garden quite soon. It's simply a wire coil stuffed with the fluff I groom out of my two furry friends. The birds will take it for their nests where it will make a lovely soft bed for their newly hatched youngsters when spring finally arrives.

Up at Blackdown Rings, an old hill fort not too far from here, at this time of year you may often spot hares in the pasture beneath the fort. I was lucky to see one last week, but although I remained still for a long time, I didn't see its mate, and eventually it lolloped away.

I first saw a hare on a smokey autumn day in Warwickshire when I was just a teenager. The cornfields had been cut and the hare rose up from the stubble only a few yards in front of me. Until then I had believed that hares were simply rabbits with longer ears, but was instantly struck by how powerful and angular these creatures are - not cuddly in the slightest, but all muscle and poised for action. No wonder that in the past they were believed to possess magical properties.

On clear days you can see for miles ...

Walking around the Iron Age ditches I noticed the gorse was coming into blossom (so kissing must be back in fashion again!) and the resident robin seemed almost to be bursting with song, even though the wind was chilly and there was a frosting of ice along the edges of the ditches

Blackdown Rings is a wonderful walk at any time of year, and on clear days you can see for miles and miles, with the countryside spread out beneath, bringing to mind that lovely poem, "The Land of Counterpane" by RL Stevenson:

"When I was sick and lay a-bed,
I had two pillows at my head,
And all my toys beside me lay,
To keep me happy all the day.

And sometimes for an hour or so
I watched my leaden soldiers go,
With different uniforms and drills,
Among the bed-clothes, through the hills;

And sometimes sent my ships in fleets
All up and down among the sheets;
Or brought my trees and houses out,
And planted cities all about.

I was the giant great and still
That sits upon the pillow-hill,
And sees before him, dale and plain,
The pleasant land of counterpane. "

Wouldn't it be a lovely idea to create a map quilt - with trees, gardens, fruit, flowers and animals stitched onto linen and mixed with carefully chosen fabrics? It would be a complicated, lengthy project, one I'd love to attempt one day, but for the moment time does not allow.

Of course there are days when time, rather than being at a premium, seems to stretch into eternity - particularly when February lives up to its name as "fill-dyke" as the rain beats on our windows and roof and the sound of running, splashing water is all around.

On days like this when their daily walk is very short and outside play is prohibited, it can be very hard to keep my canine companions amused and out of mischief - rather like having young children. When confined indoors for any length of time they will fidget and wriggle, bounce and bicker and become generally annoying, needing, like small children to be amused.

Several Christmases ago, Amy received a rather good present - K-9 Cookbook - Easy to make Dog Biscuit Recipes which are great to bake on rainy days. I first made these for Ben and Amy about five years ago, and now whenever I mention that we're going going to make dog biscuits Ben's rainy day boredom will vanish in an instant.

He heads for the kitchen, these days closely followed by his baby sister Daisy, and is immediately ready to help with measuring and mixing, patting and baking. Then of course come the tasty scrapings from the bowl while we all enjoy the savoury aromas wafting out from the oven. I am told by the Newfies that the finished biscuits are entirely delicious.

Our recipe's below if anyone wants to try for themselves ... and I don't think they'll stay in your Pet Treat tin for long!

Spot's Golden Cheese Dreams

- 3 cups (750 ml) whole wheat flour
- 2 tsps (10 ml) garlic powder
- 1/2 cup (125 ml) vegetable oil
- 1 cup (250 ml) grated (shredded) cheese
- 1 egg, beaten
- 1 cup (250 ml) milk

In a large mixing bowl, combine flour and garlic powder.

Make a well in the flour mixture and gradually stir in vegetable oil, cheese, beaten egg and milk until well blended.

Knead dough on a floured surface, about 3-4 minutes.

With a rolling pin, roll dough to 1/2" thickness.

Cut with bone-shaped biscuit cutter if you have one and place on a lightly greased baking sheet.

Bake 25 minutes at 400F 200C (we used Aga Roasting oven 3rd shelf).

Cool on rack (well out of reach!) and store in a container with loose-fitting lid.

"Goodbye rainy day blues," say Ben and Daisy, "baking is great, let's do it more often!"

Birds on a Wire

Charming and unusual way to display all manner of cherished items whether these are childrens' drawings, greetings cards, remnants of favourite fabrics - or anything you choose that can be pegged to a line.

Finished birds measure about 5 ½" from head to tail.

Making your birds:

- Fuse your piece of Bondaweb to the reverse of the fabric you've chosen for the birds' bodies.

- Peel off the backing paper and then fuse the felt backing to the reverse of the body fabric, making a sort of sandwich.

- Print and cut out the bird templates - they are given actual size. Cut 3 as given, then reverse your template for the other 3.

- Position your bird templates on the front of the fabric sandwich you just made and draw around them with the temporary fabric marker pen. You might find it easier to match their wings if you number them in some way now, then number the wings on the Bondaweb as you trace them.

- Trace the birds' wings onto Bondaweb (remember that 3 will need to be reversed) and then iron the Bondaweb to the back of your printed fabric scraps.

- Cut out the birds' wings, then peel off the paper backing and fuse the wings into place on the birds' bodies .

- You will now have six bodies ready for freestyle machine embroidery. It's much easier to stitch and then cut them out, as otherwise they're very fiddly - particularly the tails.

To make 6 birds you will need:

- 8" x 15" piece of felt or other suitable fabric for birds' bodies
- 8" x 15" piece of felt for backing
- Six printed cotton fabric scraps for wings, each measuring approx 3" x 1 ½"
- 8" x 15" piece of Bondaweb, plus small pieces for wings
- Black and yellow stranded cotton floss
- 6 wooden clothes pegs (the wooden spring clip variety)
- Temporary fabric marker pen
- Hot glue gun
- Black thread for machine needle
- Embroidery /darning foot for machine

- With black or other dark thread in your machine needle and light coloured thread in your bobbin stitch twice around the outline of each bird (just inside the outline you drew) and the wing. Remember your stitching doesn't need to be perfect - you're aiming for a sketchy, slightly scribbled sort of effect.

- Cut out birds - if your stitching was a bit wonky in places and you have to cut through it, this doesn't really matter.

- Stitch details using 1 strand of black floss for the eyes and 2 strands for the beak and feet.

- With your hot glue gun, glue a peg to the reverse of each bird.

- Finished!! Now just peg them to a line (I used jumbo ric-rac braid) to display your treasures.

Patchwork

A very Victorian trend?

In the eco-tote project on the next pages I used crazy patchwork to create the heart patch on the brown dotty eco-tote. I had a lot of fun selecting and combining some very oddly shaped scraps, and I thought it would be interesting to take a short look at the history of this thrifty technique ...

Detail from Victorian crazy patchwork tea cosy

Before the trend for crazy patchwork really took off in the mid 19th century, this technique was the preserve of the less-well off and thrifty housewife. Many different kinds of fabric - cotton, wool and linen for example, would be included in a single finished item, regardless of their shape, texture or colour. Nothing would be wasted and even the smallest scraps would find themselves being recycled to provide warm garments and bed linen. The patches were cut out, seemingly at random, but probably to avoid worn parts of the items being recycled. Sadly, but unsurprisingly, very few examples of this early form of crazy patchwork have survived.

It seems likely that better off Victorian ladies would have seen this type of work and spotted its potential for incorporating scraps of brocades, silks, satins and velvets, together with cast-off ribbons and laces into luxurious new creations. Fashions at this time were for full dresses containing yards of fabrics, opulent ball gowns and wonderfully patterned and textured interior furnishings.

However the major influence in promoting the popularity of the crazy patchwork technique is thought to have been the first official World's Fair, the Centennial Exposition, held in Philadelphia, Pennsylvania, in the year 1876, where the most popular exhibits came from Japan. "Crazed" porcelain vases with irregular shapes were greatly admired by visitors and people flocked to the Japanese stand to see the "crazed" artwork. Needlewomen who admired these vases then began to interpret the lines of the crazed and crackled finish of the Japanese porcelain in the irregular outlines of their crazy patchwork and so a new trend began.

Stitchers would take great care to plan their work carefully, as the Victorian method of crazy patchwork meant there was enormous potential for creative expression in the shapes and sizes of patches as well as the almost limitless choice of embellishments available.

Patterns and templates weren't used in crazy patchwork, as the patches were freely cut in asymmetrical shapes and then stitched to a foundation fabric to fit in with adjoining patches. After this process was completed, the seams were elaborately embroidered with a colourful and, to modern eyes, gaudy variety of threads and stitches. Then the whole work was embellished with whatever the seamstress had to hand - buttons and bows, silk flowers, ribbons, lace, beads and even feathers. She might also decide to record important events and anniversaries by embroidering names, dates and perhaps including scraps from a Christening robe or another garment worn to an important event, so her finished item would have had real emotional value.

Many beautiful embroidered motifs of animals and flowers were stitched in the centres of some of the patches and women who were talented in decorative painting would sometimes paint images onto their crazy quilts. Finished crazy quilts were never intended as utilitarian quilts. Their sole purpose was to show off the maker's embroidery skills and to decorate the home.

Crazy patchwork bag kit from Crazy Creation, Devon
www.crazycreation.co.uk

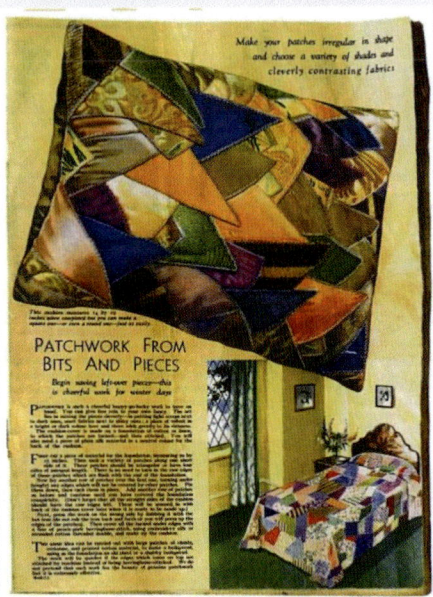

Mid 20th century magazine project

The crazy patchwork trend was relatively short lived, fading in the 1920s and early 1930s when it lost much of the lavish Victorian style and decoration. Fabrics became less luxurious and designs less well - crazy! There was a limited revival in the 1950s and 60s, perhaps influenced by the popularity of crazy paving in towns and gardens, but designs were much simpler. Fewer embellishments were used and more use was made of the sewing machine. Of course by this time many sewing machines were able to offer decorative stitches, which made an attractive substitute for the traditional hand embroidering of the patchwork seams.

Today this fun and just a little crazy technique is enjoying a revival with fresh and innovative ideas and creative use of the wonderful range of fabrics and delightful kits now available.

Three Patchwork Eco-totes

Doing your bit for the environment is fun with these three cute tote bags. Simple to make, but definitely not ordinary with the addition of your choice of three patchwork designs to applique to the front of your bag.

Choose from Stitch and Flip bird, Crazy Patchwork heart or Hexie Bunny.

All three tote bags are made in the same way, so I have started with the instructions to make your basic bag. I have made my handles long enough to go over my shoulder (as my hands are usually full of dogs' leads and other shopping!), but this is personal preference and it's easy to alter the handle lengths if you wish.

The detailed instructions for creating your applique shapes follow after the tote bag instructions. Seam allowance is ¼" except where stated otherwise.

To make one basic tote you will need:

- Three rectangles of medium-weight cotton fabric - one measuring 32" x 16" and the other two each measuring 28" x 2"

To make your basic tote:

- Take your larger rectangle of fabric and fold it in half along the longer side, so you have a square of fabric with 16" sides.

- Press the fold. This will be the bottom of your bag

- **NOW APPLY YOUR CHOSEN APPLIQUE DESIGN to the front of the bag. You should position it centrally vertically and between 3 and 4" up from the fold you have just pressed into your fabric.**

- With *right* sides together join the side seams of your bag.

- Turn your bag inside out and press the seams carefully.

- Now stitch down each side again ½" from the previous seam. This makes a French seam - a folded pocket that hides the raw edge of the fabric.

- Still with your bag inside out press the seams again.

- Now turn over the top of the back, first ¼ and then ½" and press. Pin or tack if liked, then stitch all the way around the top.

- Turn bag right way round and press. The main part of your bag is now finished.

- Now make the handles. Take your two long thin rectangles and fold in half lengthways, right side inwards, then press firmly.

- Stitch across one short end, then all down one long side.

- Push the blunt end of a knitting needle or other long thin object up into the tube of fabric - because you stitched across one short end the needle won't slide straight through, but will push the tube through itself, turning it right-side out.

- When turned out, press your handle - the seam should run down one side. If you experience difficulties flattening it for pressing, roll the seam between your finger and thumb - this will turn and flatten it.

- Top stitch the full length of your handle ¼" from the seamed edge.

- Turn under the unfinished edge of your handle and press. Repeat with the other handle.

- Pin handles into place at top of bag and machine stitch to bag.

  • Stitching in a crossed rectangle is nice and strong.

  Your basic tote bag is now finished.

Hexie Bunny Shape

You will need:

- 12" square piece of white or pale coloured medium to lightweight cotton or poly-cotton fabric.
- Assortment of fabric scraps sufficient to cut approx 20 hexagons measuring 3" w x 2 5/8" high with sides of 1 ½"
- Sharpie or other thick felt tip pen
- Temporary fabric spray adhesive
- Darning/embroidery foot for your sewing machine (optional)
- Cream and black thread for needle, cream or other light-coloured thread for bobbin.

To make your bunny:

- Cut out the rabbit shape template (given actual size, though you can enlarge or reduce if preferred - don't forget that doing this will alter the number of hexagons you will need).
- Iron your white fabric and place it on a clean flat surface.
- Draw around the edge of the template onto the fabric with your sharpie or felt tip pen.
- Make sure the ink has bled through so that your lines can be seen from the other side of the fabric - this is very important.
- Cut your hexagons from your scraps of fabric. You will need approximately 20, but this may vary depending upon how you decide to position them on your bunny outline.
- Spray the bunny shape with temporary fabric adhesive and begin to cover it with cut out hexagons, butting them up well against each other.

- Continue in this way until you have covered all the shapes. Pat your hexagons down well to make sure they're properly adhered to the fabric base.
- You should still be able to see the outline of your bunny shape on the other side when you flip the fabric over
- Set your sewing machine to a wide, short zigzag stitch - rather as though you were going to stitch a buttonhole - though the stitch length can be a little longer than for buttonholes.
- Stitch all along the edges of the hexagons, securing them to the fabric below. Make sure your zigzag is wide enough to catch in the hexagons on either side of the join. Continue until you've stitched all the hexagons to your base fabric.

- Turn your work over and, with a straight machine stitch stitch all around the edge of the shape just inside the lines you drew. This will keep the hexagons firmly in place when you cut out.

- Cut out your bunny shape.

- Position on tote bag panel (see instructions on page 2) and secure with temporary fabric spray adhesive.

- Drop the feed dogs on your sewing machine and fit darning foot. With black thread in your needle and cream in your bobbin stitch around the edge of the bunny twice to secure him firmly to your bag. You want a sort of scribbled effect - not too neat.

- If you prefer not to use freehand machine stitching, then you can secure him with a zigzag stitch or simply topstitch him to the bag panel.

- Now complete your tote following the instructions on page 2.

Crazy Heart Shape

You will need:

- 12" square piece of lightweight white or pale coloured cotton or poly-cotton fabric

- Assortment of fabric scraps with at least one straight edge- I chose shades of pink for my heart

- Pinking shears (optional)

- Temporary spray fabric adhesive

- Embroidery/darning foot for sewing machine (optional), black and cream thread for needle, light coloured thread in bobbin

To make your heart shape:

- Cut out a heart shape - I haven't provided a template as these are so easily found. It should be about 10" from top to bottom.

- Iron your white fabric and place it on a clean flat surface.

- Draw around the edge of the template onto the fabric with your sharpie or felt tip pen.

- Make sure the ink has bled through so that your lines can be seen from the other side of the fabric - this is very important.

- Decide which scrap will be your first piece and cut it so it has 5 straight edges. It doesn't have to be any particular shape just one that is pleasing to your eye as this will be the foundation piece for your crazy patchwork.

- Spray a little adhesive onto the reverse of this scrap and position it on your heart right side up. Pat down to hold it securely in place. It doesn't have to be exactly in the centre, but you will need to have space all around it.

- Take another scrap and lay it right side down down on top of the first piece lining up one of the straight edges.

- Pin the second scrap in place in place and sew a 1/4" seam down the lined up edge through both the foundation piece.

- Press the seam open so the piece lies flat on your base fabric. You can spray a little adhesive on the reverse if you wish to secure it in place as you work on different parts of your heart.

- Move to another side of your foundation piece and repeat, you may find yourself covering up some of the other piece of fabric - that's absolutely fine.

- Continue working around that first piece layering and sewing. Use different shapes and size scraps as you go to create an interesting pattern. Continue this way until your whole heart shape is covered.

- Press, then flip your work over and machine stitch all around heart just inside the line you drew with your felt tip pen. This will keep all the patches in place when you cut your heart out.

- Cut your heart out - I used pinking shears for a nice decorative effect - but this is optional.

- If liked, use some of the decorative stitches on your machine to mimic the hand embellishment used on many crazy patchwork designs. You could choose different coloured threads to contrast with your fabric choices, but I just used cream.

- Position on tote bag panel (see instructions on page 2) and secure with temporary fabric spray adhesive.

- Drop the feed dogs on your sewing machine and fit darning foot. With black thread in your needle and cream in your bobbin stitch around the edge of the heart twice to secure it firmly to your bag. You want a sort of scribbled effect - not too neat.

- If you prefer not to use freehand machine stitching, then you can simply topstitch it to the bag panel.

- Now complete your tote following the instructions on page 2.

Bird in Flight Shape

You will need:

- 12" square piece of lightweight white or pale coloured cotton or poly-cotton fabric
- Strips of scrap fabric of varying widths
- Sharpie or other thick felt tip pen
- Temporary fabric spray adhesive
- Darning/embroidery foot for your sewing machine (optional)
- Cream and black thread for needle, cream or other light-coloured thread for bobbin.

To make your bird:

- Cut out the bird shape template (given actual size, though you can enlarge or reduce if preferred).
- Iron your white fabric and place it on a clean flat surface.
- Draw around the edge of the template onto the fabric with your sharpie or felt tip pen.
- Make sure the ink has bled through so that your lines can be seen from the other side of the fabric - this is very important.
- Lay your first strip of fabric right side up across the top wing and tail of the bird as shown in the photograph, securing with a little spray adhesive.
- Take your next strip of fabric and place right side down aligning the two long sides. Machine into place with a ¼" seam.

- Flip the second strip of fabric over and press down.
- Repeat with subsequent strips of fabric until your bird shape is covered.
- Press, then turn over and machine stitch all around the edge of your bird just inside the felt tip lines you drew. Cut bird shape out along lines.

- Position on tote bag panel (see instructions on page 2) and secure with temporary fabric spray adhesive.
- Drop the feed dogs on your sewing machine and fit darning foot. With black thread in your needle and cream in your bobbin stitch around the edge of the heart twice to secure it firmly to your bag. You want a sort of scribbled effect - not too neat.
- If you prefer not to use freehand machine stitching, then you can simply topstitch it to the bag panel.
- Now complete your tote following the instructions on page 2.

Really Easy Fabric-covered Lampshades

After we installed our new wood-burning stove at Coombe Leigh before Christmas (very toasty toes) we needed to decorate the room as the alterations needed had left it looking definitely the worse for wear!

Our existing table lamp was fine, but the shade was looking a bit tired, suffering from years of service and enhanced by a nice mud splatter from the time Ben dashed in from his walk and shook himself vigorously before I had time to catch him! Rather than go to the expense of purchasing a brand-new shade I decided to use this easy technique to give the old shade a whole new look - and was so pleased with the results I thought I'd share how I did it.

The fabric you choose shouldn't be too heavy if you want plenty of light to filter through - I used a quilting weight cotton - and for the best effect try to relate the scale of the pattern on your fabric to the size of the lampshade you're covering.

You will need:

- Smooth paper of fabric lampshade
- Newspaper to make template
- Sufficient fabric to cover shade (about ½ yard for an average sized shade, but you will be able to see exactly when you've drawn your template)
- Fabric or PVA glue
- Pencil
- Scissors

To make your shade:

- First make your template: Place the shade, seam down, on your piece of newspaper and mark the top and base seam position on the paper. Starting from the seam and tracing around the base with your pencil, gently roll the shade until you reach the seam again.

This is a really easy and quick technique - a great way to use a special piece of fabric - and you don't need to sew a single stitch!

- Roll your shade back along this traced line, this time marking the paper along the top edge. Cut out your paper pattern.

- Before you continue, double-check that it fits properly. Wrap your paper template around the shade and check all is well. Make any adjustments to the template that are needed.

- Place your template on your fabric and draw around it, adding a 1" seam allowance to the curved edges and ¼ to the straight ends.

- Turn under and press a ¼" turning on one straight edge of your fabric.

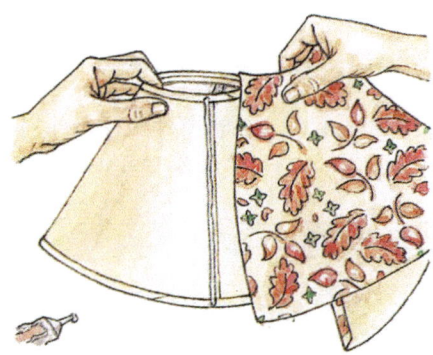

- Apply a thin line of glue along the seam of the lampshade. Position the raw edge of your fabric on the glued line, centering the edge on the seam so that the fabric overlaps the shade edges by ½" at the top and bottom.

- Apply a thin line of glue along the top and base edges of the shade.

- Working from the glued end, smooth the fabric around the shade, making sure it is firmly stuck down on the rims. Stop 1" from the glued end.

- Squeeze a thin line of glue on top of the raw edge of fabric where you began and then smooth down the turned edge to cover the raw edge and allow the whole shade to dry.

- You may or may not need to clip the excess fabric before you glue it to the reverse of the shade. Try folding it down with your fingers first to see if it sits comfortably or whether the edge does need to be clipped.

- Clip if necessary.

- Apply a little glue to the reverse of the excess fabric at the top and bottom edges of the shade.

- Fold the fabric to the inside of the shade and press down firmly.

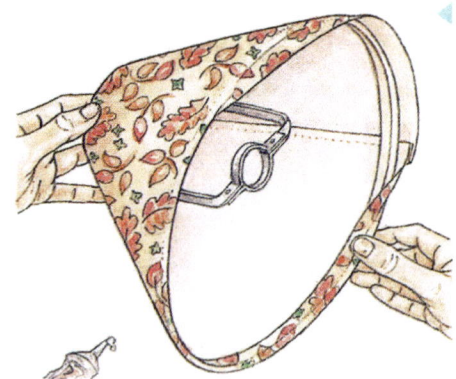

FINISHED!!

Nobody needs reminding that February 14th is St Valentine's day ....

Yes, February 14th is a special day for lovers, when romance is most definitely in the air - and hopefully in the post(!) ... but who was St Valentine and how did it all begin?

Nearly 2,000 years ago in ancient Rome, February 14th was the day dedicated to the goddess Juno, the deity of women and marriage. Valentine was an early Christian bishop who would marry young couples in secret, defying the Emperor Claudius who had forbidden such ceremonies. Eventually Valentine was caught conducting a secret marriage ceremony and condemned to be put to death.

Whilst he was in prison awaiting his execution, many young couples were able to toss small gifts of flowers, food and other tokens of their appreciation through his cell window. Eventually Valentine's execution date arrived - the fourteenth of February AD 270, and as he waited to be taken out to die, the Bishop sent a final message to the young woman he loved - signing it simply "from your Valentine."

In he year 496 AD, Pope Gelasius chose Bishop Valentine as the patron saint of lovers, who would be honoured on the fourteenth of every February. Over the years, Valentine's Day has evolved into a holiday when gifts, cards, flowers and chocolates are given to those we love or would like to start a relationship with. And it is all because of a long ago Roman Bishop named Valentine.

Over the centuries many Valentine legends have evolved, and the theme of this month's magazine was inspired by the old English tradition - that February 14th is the day that birds fall in love and choose their mates .....

Owls in Love Cushion Cover

Nine cute little owls - and two who simply can't take their eyes off each other!

Sized to fit 16" square cushion pad

To make a 16" cover you will need:

- Blanket pieces or other woollen fabric: One piece 16" square and two pieces 16" x 12"
- 3 x 9" square felt for owl bodies – colours toffee, oak and caramel
- 2 x 6" square felt for owl spectacles – colours mushroom and skintone
- 6" square felt for owl eyes – colour buttermilk
- Small scrap of red felt for heart
- Scraps of fabric for owl breasts
- 18 small buttons (9 matching pairs) for centres of eyes – or if you are making for a child's room then substitute buttons with small circles of felt.
- Gold embroidery floss for beaks and feet
- Dark brown, dark red and very pale green embroidery floss
- Spray fabric adhesive or Bondaweb
- Pinking shears

Make your applique panel:

Make your owls up before attaching them to the front of your cushion pad.

- Cut out 7 ordinary owls and 2 owls with wing outstretched from felt, reversing your template so the wings are on opposite sides of the owls
- Cut out spectacles and eyes from felt and breasts from your fabric scraps. Cut along the base edge of the breast piece with pinking shears if you have them as this will give a nice feather effect on your finished owls.
- Take the square piece of your woollen fabric and fold it into three equal parts both vertically and horizontally. Press lightly, then open out. Your fabric will now be divided into 9 equal-sized squares by the creases you have created.
- Place one owl in each square using the photo at the top of the pattern. Do not attach them to the base fabric. You are positioning them at this stage to help you choose how to position their breasts, spectacles and eyes.
- Position breasts, spectacles, eyes and buttons on owls, playing around with them until you are happy with their arrangement. If you are using different designs of fabric for the breasts, then take your time at this stage to make sure you've chosen the best combination of fabrics.

- When you are happy with your arrangement, take each owl in turn and attach first the breast and then the spectacles using spray fabric adhesive. The spectacles should cover the raw edge at the top of the breast.
- Straight machine stitch along the base of the owl just inside the pinked edge, then machine zig-zag over the raw edges of the sides of the breasts and straight around the spectacles and zig-zag down the second side of the breast. You don't need to fully stitch around the bottom of the spectacles as these will be attached when you add the beak.

- Attach the eyes using spray adhesive and then using golden embroidery floss (6 strands) attach the buttons for the pupils. The template shows the buttons in the centre, but they actually look best slightly off centre (same in both eyes or your owl will be crosseyed!). Make sure the two love birds are looking at each other! (See photos for guide)

- Stitch the felt eye circles to the spectacles as shown using three strands of pale green floss. Stitch the beak and feet using six strands of gold floss.

- Attach your finished owls to the front panel using spray adhesive or Bondaweb.

- Then stitch around the edges using small straight stitches at right-angles to the owl shape and three strands of dark brown floss. Make the stitches a little longer at the base of the breasts to look like feathers.

- Stitch the wings on the love birds in the same way and add some back-stitching for feathers (see photographs)

- Attach the loveheart between the two owls as shown in the photographs.

Make up your cushion cover:

- Press lightly on the reverse of your applique panel to press out your guideline creases.

- Hem one long edge of each of the back pieces.

- Place your front panel right side up on a clean flat surface, then place your back pieces on top, aligning the sides and with the hemmed edges overlapping at the centre and pin or stitch in place.

- Machine stitch twice (for strength) around the edges of the cushion pad ½" in from the edge. Make your corners rounded to allow for the thickness of the fabric when turning. (Your cover will be slightly smaller than your pad size which will make for a plump cushion and also allow for the pad flattening slightly with use).

- Turn right side out and insert pad.

- ADMIRE!

OWL TEMPLATES

Cut 7 owl bodies without wing (ie along dotted line)

Cut 1 owl body with wing on right then reverse template and cut 1 owl body with wing on left side.

SPECTACLES
cut one for each owl

CHEST
Cut one for each owl

Cut bottom using pinking shears

Made for Each Other

When I was a child I had a book about a little hedgehog who was lonely and unloved because her prickles hurt anyone who came too close. In the end she did find love … with a turtle who didn't mind her spikey body. Memories of that book have inspired the embroidery on this heart, showing the little hedgehog snuggled up against her true love.

Filled with lavender this heart would make a perfect gift for a loved one, or maybe a wedding favour? It's really easy to make and the embroidery is very simple ….

You will need:

- 2 x 10" square (28 cm square) linen
- Stranded cotton floss in light brown and pink
- Dried lavender
- Polyfil
- 6" (15 cm) ribbon for hanging

Method:

- Transfer the embroidery pattern, shown actual size, onto the centre one of the linen squares (fold in 4 and where the creases cross is the centre)
- Using two strands of floss, work the design in back stitch for the outlines and short straight stitch for the hedgehog's prickles
- Use long and short stitch to embroider the heart.
- The cheeks are worked freehand in satin stitch.
- Wash your fabric if necessary to remove the transfer lines. Iron on the reverse.
- Cut out two heart shapes from the linen. Place right sides together and position ribbon at top of heart as shown .
- Pin and stitch the pieces together leaving a 2" (5 cm) gap for turning.

- Trim closely at point of heart (careful not to cut stitches) and clip the curves at the top. Turn right side out and press.
- Stuff with polyfil at the top of the heart to give it a nice rounded shape and fill the bottom part with lavender.
- Hand stitch the gap you left for turning closed and hang.

Made for each other

Made for each other

Transferring Your Pattern

Possibly the most frequent query I receive is "How do I transfer my embroidery design from the printed page to my fabric?"

This is one of those questions where there isn't a single right or wrong answer – it's all about choosing the method that works best for you.

The easiest method to transfer a design is of course an iron-on transfer, many of which used to be given away free with needlework magazines in the mid-20th century, printed in either blue or silver.

My grandmother had a huge collection of these transfers, all carefully stored in a biscuit box with a cute puppy and kitten picture on the lid. There were sunbonnet and crinoline ladies - too many to count - birds, bears and an infinite variety of flower patterns. If you enjoy stitching vintage, it's still easy to find these old designs in thrift shops, at jumble sales and of course on auction sites such as eBay.

But if you don't have a transfer and want to transfer a downloaded pattern (like those in this magazine) there are several different methods available to you, some of which are easier, and so perhaps more popular, than others.

If you're embroidering onto a pale coloured, light-weight fabric, then it's easy to trace your design onto it as though it was tracing paper. To do this, print your design in the usual way, then tape your printed sheet to a light source - most usually a light box or window pane. Position your fabric over it, right side up, making sure that the design is beneath the position you have chosen for your finished embroidery.

Tape your fabric in place over the paper. Don't be tempted to try to hold it with one hand while tracing with the other - unless it's really small and simple your fabric is quite likely to slip out of position leading to frustration and a spoiled design (I am speaking from experience!). If you have some then masking tape is the best to use as it's easier to remove than sellotape and leaves less sticky residue. Use the smallest amount you actually need and keep it to the edges of your fabric, just in case.

When everything is securely held in place, trace over your design with a sharp pencil or a water soluble temporary fabric marker pen. I have read debate online about whether or not the marks from these pens can reappear over a period of time, spoiling your finished work. I haven't personally experienced this problem, but if in doubt then use a pencil. This will leave a permanent mark, but it won't bleed into other areas and should be covered by your stitching.

Another popular choice is to use dressmakers' carbon paper. This isn't at all the same as the old-fashioned carbon paper those of us of a certain age remember using when typing copies of a letter on a typewriter. *(Aside: Did you know that typewriters are no longer manufactured anywhere in the world?)* Dressmakers' carbon paper is a thicker, waxier paper and doesn't smudge. It is available in different colours to suit different fabrics. This technique is only good for smooth fabrics.

Iron the fabric you want to stitch on and then place it right side up on a clean flat surface. Tape it securely to the surface. Choose the best colour carbon paper to show up on this fabric and tape this into place shiny side down. Then position your pattern on top of the carbon paper and again, tape (or pin) it to stop it slipping around as you work. Then take a pencil or ballpoint pen and draw carefully over the lines of the pattern.

Don't press too hard or you might tear the paper and spoil the design, but press firmly enough for your lines to show up on the fabric. You might want to test this first on a corner of the fabric. Once you've traced over all the lines, remove the tape and lift off the pattern and carbon paper - your design will then be ready to stitch.

You can also purchase transfer pencils - the lines these draw will iron onto your fabric in the same way as the old-fashioned transfers. For this method you will need to print the reversed pattern. Then on your printed sheet, draw over the pattern lines with the transfer pen. The sheet can then be turned over and the design ironed onto your fabric - when of course it will be the right way round.

Prick and pounce is a time-honoured method that sounds like some kind of old-fashioned music hall act - in fact it's a very old tried and trusted method of transferring a design to fabric. It does take a little while, but is very effective. The pounce is a powder which comes in either black (crushed charcoal) or white (powdered cuttlefish - yes really!) - or you can mix the two to make grey.

You can purchase a special pad to apply the pounce, or make your own from a rolled up piece of felt. Then trace your design onto tracing paper and lay it on a folded cloth or ironing board. With a hat pin, pin in cork, or even another special tool you can purchase just for this purpose, prick a series of small holes closely together all along the design lines. Then tape your fabric onto a flat board or working surface and tape the pricked tracing paper onto the fabric. Dip your pad into the pounce powder and, with a circular motion, gently rub the pounce over the design.

Complete the whole design before removing the pricked tracing paper in a single nice clean

movement. If you brush the pounce from the pricked paper it can be reused indefinitely. Now, following the pounce outline, paint a fine line all along the dotted outlines on the fabric, using a brush and watercolour paint, or very fine marker. Then un-tape and shake your fabric to remove the pounce.

Tacking through tissue paper is another a time-honoured, fairly time consuming, method of transferring your design. It is great in that it leaves absolutely no marks on your fabric and is suitable for all kinds of fabric.

Carefully trace your design onto tissue paper. Then position your tracing on top of the fabric and secure in place around the edges. Tack around the outline starting and finishing your line securely. Make sure the stitches are not too small or they will be hard to remove, and not too big so that you miss parts of the design.

Once you've stitched over the whole design, carefully tear away the tissue paper, leaving the tacking on the fabric. (you can also buy water soluble paper to help in this stage). If you're working on a light or delicate fabric, then be very very careful when removing the paper so you don't damage the fabric. The tacking stitch outline can be removed as you progress, or after the embroidery is completed.

My favourite way is to print the design in reverse using my laser printer. Then I use heat to transfer the design to my fabric. I have an old heat press that is great for this as it applies the heat evenly and the press holds everything in place securely. This method only works for cotton and linen fabrics though as I have found that for the best results the transfer time needs to be in excess of 40 seconds and it requires a temperature of 195 degrees, so there is always a danger of scorching.

I don't know if this would be possible with an iron and would hesitate to recommend this method - but if you have access to a heat press and laser printer then you could experiment - once you've found the ideal settings it's a great method as even the tiniest details can be transferred without difficulty.

If you have successfully used another method, or have any hints you'd like to share then please do let me know so I can pass them on to Bustle & Sew readers. Meanwhile … happy stitching!

Sparrows are vintage Bestway transfers

Vintage Pattern: Moonlight Capers

This pattern was published in the May 1952 issue of "Stitchcraft." The instructions are quite detailed, with little diagrams for the needlelace details. I think the design would also lend itself well to applique. It's the little details that I like best, such as the two inquisitive bunnies wondering what is happening on this starlight night!

"Moonlight Capers"

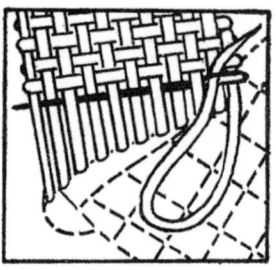

BOY'S JACKET

Following in the footsteps of 'Arry and 'Arriet, Country Cousins, Angus My Own and so on, comes this charming country pair "gathering peascods" with all their heart and soul, the kitten and moths join in, and the rabbits look on in surprise. I am afraid all the earlier designs in this series are absolutely out of print, but we hope to reprint 'Arry and 'Arriet later on this year.

• • •

Materials: Piece of natural linen, 24 × 18 inches. 7 skeins Beehive Tapestry Wool—1 each black 52, emerald 1710, royal blue 1722, yellow 1801, blue 1720, cherry 1703 and tan 1838.

Stranded cottons as follows:—1 skein each of black, white, and fawn; scraps of brown, dark grey, light grey, leaf green, jade, orange, gold, red and pale blue.

Transfer No. 458, price 9d. post-free from STITCHCRAFT Ltd., Great West Road, Brentford, Middlesex. The actual design measures 20 inches wide by 12½ inches deep, including the stars, so the coloured illustration, which is not quite complete, is about half life-size.

EMBROIDERY

Iron off transfer. The panel is worked mainly in wools with touches of cotton for fine detail and highlights (figures in brackets indicate number of cotton strands to be used).

GIRL. Jacket: Darned solidly in black wool (see diagram for boy's jacket); linings, blue satin-stitch. Skirt: lines of stem in royal blue, cherry, emerald and yellow; frills, white darning (6 strands); lower edge, black wool buttonhole. Jumper: neck, white buttonhole (6); front, white chain-stitch (6); belt, cherry satin.

Cap: royal blue darning; pom-pom, cherry satin. Fingers, thumbs and linings: white satin (6); hands, white buttonhole to imitate crochet (2). Stockings: stripes, cherry stem-stitch; outline, black stem (2). Boots: darned in black wool; laces, black stem (1); soles, brown stem outline for one, brown satin for the other (6).

Face and neck: outlined black stem (2); strands of hair, fawn stem (1); plaits, fawn double back-stitch (2); bows, pale blue satin (2); cheeks, criss-cross lines of orange (1); mouth, orange satin (2); eyes, white and pale blue (2), eyelashes, brows and nose, black (1).

BOY. Jacket: royal blue darning, right arm underlined with a line of black wool; linings, light grey satin (6). Scarf: cherry satin with emerald, black and yellow stripes and cherry straight stitches for fringe. Jersey: yellow chain; hem, black satin. Cap: crown, darned with white and tan for checks; peak, tan satin with underside in black. Features as for girl; hair, 1 strand of fawn straight stitches.

Trousers: laid filling of fawn cotton (3), outlined tan wool stem-stitch; strings at knee, gold stem (2). Socks: yellow chain-stitch. Shoes: black wool satin with brown satin soles (6); strings in 1 strand of black. Whistle: 2 lines of fawn stem (6); hands, black stem (2). Bird: black and orange satin (both 2); eye, in white and beak in gold (both 2).

Lines in foreground: light grey stem, 6 strands for

• *this lovable pair of country bumpkins makes a delightfully amusing contemporary wall panel*

PANEL lines in front, 3 for lines behind. Post on right: outlined, black stem (2); flower, red detached chain (6); stem and leaves in jade (3). Rabbits: straight stitches down backs, satin-stitch ears and stem-stitch round faces and fronts, all in 2 strands of fawn; tails, white (2); eyes, white satin, outlined black (3); grass, leaf-green straight sts. (3) and stem (6).

Kitten: outlined dark grey straight stitches and stem (2); ears, dark grey satin (2); eyes, white, outlined black (2); nose, black satin (2); whiskers, black (1). Large moth: wings, white long and short with dark grey inside (2); body, black straight stitches (2); head, French knot (1); antennae, black straight stitches (1). Small moths: wings, white detached chain stitches (1); one detached chain for body and one black French knot for head (1). Grass: leaf-green buttonhole (6). Moon: white stem (6). Stars: white straight stitches radiating from centre (6) with a longer stitch between each (1).

Press finished embroidery lightly on wrong side under a damp cloth.

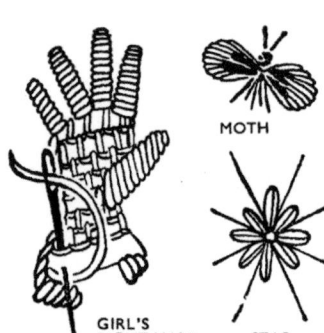

GIRL'S RIGHT HAND   MOTH   STAR

Daisy Knot Bag

Cheerful little bag that's so easy to make with no complicated zips or poppers to insert. The simple daisy applique design makes this easy pattern into something just a little bit special - and perfect for those warmer days of spring and summer.

Finished bag measures 9 ½ " high x 7" diameter base (approx)

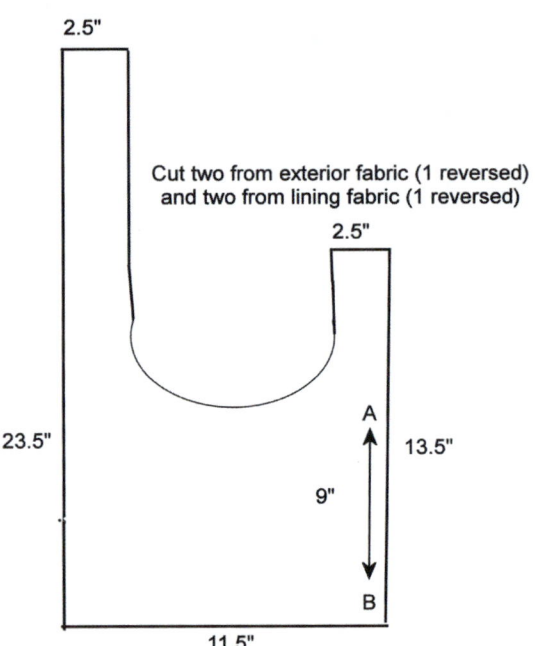

Cut two from exterior fabric (1 reversed) and two from lining fabric (1 reversed)

You will need:

- ½ yard heavy weight fabric for bag exterior
- ½ yard quilting weight fabric for lining
- 12 x 18" piece of white felt
- 9" square yellow felt
- Scraps of green felt in 3 different shades for leaves
- Newspaper to draw pattern
- Green, black and cream thread for machine needle, cream or other light colour for bobbin
- Darning/embroidery foot for sewing machine
- Bondaweb

Note: Seam allowance is ¼" throughout

Cut your pieces:

- Using the diagram above draw the template for your bag shape onto your newspaper. Also draw a 7" diameter circle for the bag base.
- Cut the main bag pieces and also 2 pieces for the base - one from your lining and one from your exterior fabric.

Applique Panel:

- Join your two exterior pieces from A to B (ie 9" up from the base of the bag) and press seam flat.
- Using the diagram on the next page as a guide, draw 12 daisy shapes, 12 daisy centres and 21 leaf shapes onto the paper side of your Bondaweb. The daisies vary between 2" and 3" in diameter and are very simple - just like the flowers we all used to draw as children!
- Iron the Bondaweb onto your felt, then cut out the shapes and peel off the paper backing.
- Position your applique shapes onto your bag panel using the diagram on the next page as a guide. The bottom of the applique should be no closer than 1" to the bottom of your exterior fabric. Remember that you will need ¼" seam allowance on each end to join your panel, so do not position your applique shapes too close to the ends.
- When you're happy with your applique, iron the felt shapes onto the fabric. I usually cover felt with a muslin cloth before pressing felt to avoid flattening, scorching or marking it.

Do not iron down your shapes until you're happy with the positioning. Overlap some leaves with the daisy shapes.

- Fit the darning/embroidery foot to your machine and drop the feed dogs. With green thread in your needle and cream/light coloured thread in your bobbin, stitch twice around each daisy shape and twice around each centre. Your stitching shouldn't be too neat, you are aiming for a sort of scribbled effect.

- Then change to black in your needle and stitch twice around the edge of the leaves, and down the middle of each leaf to represent the veins.

- Make the centre stitching a bit wobbly on either side as though smaller veins were branching out from the centre.

- Turn your panel over and press lightly on the reverse. Your applique is now finished.

Assemble your bag:

- Fold your exterior panel in half along the seam you joined at the beginning and sew the side seam in the same way as the first side (ie from A to B again).

- Insert the circular base.

- Repeat these steps with the lining fabric, but joining the lining on both sides from A to B.

- You will now have two pieces that look like bags, but without the handles joined.

- Insert the bag exterior bag into the lining with the right sides facing.

- Sew the outer fabric and the lining together along the sides of the handles and the curve at the top of the bag to within 2" of the top of each handle. (This feels very odd, but it will work out in the end!)

- Turn the bag right-side out through the top of one handle.

- Join the handles at the top of the lining and exterior seams.

- Turn the side seams under and press well.

- Top stitch all around the handles and the curve at the top of the bag, this will hold everything in place.

- Press along seams. Your bag is now finished.

Hints and Tips from Stitchers

Some time ago I asked blog readers about their favourite stitching tips. They responded very generously - and I received an enormous number of tips ranging from the seemingly sensible to the weird and wacky! On trying them out, every single one worked, so I thought it would be fun to share a few here too.

If you have any tips you'd like to share with other readers then please do email me helen@bustleandsew.com so I can include them in future issues:

"I keep several needles going at the same time and it's a trial trying to remember which colour is which. So I fold a piece of felt, 9" x 12" into quarters and tack it together. Then I put a piece of clear packing tape down the centre. Now I write the colour number and symbol if need be on small labels and stick them to the tape in two rows. I have been able to put up to 22 colours on my needle keeper at a time. I keep several of these around so when I want to start a new project I already have a needle keeper ready"

Kate Roland

http:crazypurplemom.blogspot.com

"Just a little thing really, when threading your needle, hold the thread between your thumb and forefinger, have just a little peeking out - about ¼" then lower the needle onto the thread - works every time for me. I was given this advice by a lady from the W.I. years ago."

Lesleyann Bradford

"Always have your thread no longer than the length between your elbow and the tip of your finger. This avoids thread knotting up."

Ann Brown

http://anniebhandmade.blogspot.com

"To separate your stranded embroidery threads (eg DMC), cut thread to length. Hold threads about 1 cm (just under ½") from the top. Separate them a little and take hold of one thread. Gently pull it out of the bundle with one hand, while still holding the rest of the threads in the other hand. You will need to then run your fingers down the rest of the threads to straighten them. Repeat for each single thread you need. This stops all the tangling up of the threads when separating them."

Christine MacDonald

http:macdonaldspatch.blogspot.com

"This may be something that everybody already knows, but when my mother taught me to embroider, she explained what, for me, has been a very helpful tip. When you're having trouble getting your needle to come up in just the right spot - for example when working extremely small stitches, or when the canvas is already quite crowded and you can't see well or stitch without catching other threads accidentally, stick your needle in from the top of the fabric where you can see exactly where you're putting it and wiggle it around for a moment. Then take it back out again without making a stitch. When you remove it the hole you've made will stay open long enough for you to take the needle round to the back again and poke it up through the hole at exactly the right spot."

Cecilia

"I know this is very basic, but I like to press the fabric flat before placing it in a hoop. I have better luck with smoother stitches. I don't use starch or sizing on it, just a good pressing to smooth out any wrinkles in the fabric."

Linda

Mice are Nice Embroidery

Three endearing little mice decorate two verses of Rose Fylman's delightful poem "I think mice are rather nice." Certainly these little embroidered mice are rather nice - and won't be nibbling things they shouldn't touch anytime soon.

Finished design measures 7 ¾" x 10 ½"

You will need:

- 12" x 14" piece of material suitable for embroidering on (I used a vintage eiderdown fabric). It should be non-stretchy and made from cotton, linen or a blend of the two fibres. This design looks good if you choose a fabric with a simple print as the palette used in the actual stitching is quite limited, the print will make the finished work "sparkle".
- DMC stranded cotton floss in colours 310, 746, 945, 3021, 3750, 3782, 3790, 3864

General notes on stitching:

- Stitches used are long & short stitch, straight stitch, back stitch, stem stitch, satin stitch and French knots.
- The transfers are given at 70% of actual size
- Two strands of floss are used throughout *except for whiskers and the shadow line beneath feet and tails when one strand was used.*
- The eyes are stitched in satin stitch 310, with a tiny stitch in a single strand of 746 to add sparkle.
- Two shades of pink are used for paws, ears, tails and noses. Use the darker shade (3864) where there would be shadows, ie bottom edge of tail, bottoms of paws and base of ears, and blend in the lighter shade where more light would fall on a real mouse.
- The text is stitched in backstitch in 2 strands of 3750. When working text be very precise with your back stitch, ensuring that your needle goes up and down through the fabric in the same hole so your words will have a nice smooth line. Your stitches won't be all the same size, make them shorter to fit around curves. If there is a choice between one slightly longer stitch and two shorter ones, always make them shorter.

Notes on stitching fur:

There are just two important things to remember when stitching fur - firstly the direction in which the fur lies, and secondly the contours and shading of the animal - or where the fur will be lighter or darker due to shadowed areas.

I have seen animals with fur stitched around their eyes in circles - this is quite wrong and doesn't look at all natural. If you have a pet then look carefully at him or her and notice the direction in which the fur grows. ALWAYS away from the nose. The nose is the focus of all your fur. And look at how their fur overlaps so that fur nearest the nose lies on top of fur further down the body. To achieve this effect you need to decide how the fur would lie on the animal you are stitching:

Arrows indicate direction of fur

IIt is a good idea to stitch the tail and paws in pink first (I didn't do this with the mouse I'm going to show you in stages, and had to go back and add extra stitches). If you do this then you can overlap the end of your pink stitching with fur stitches - just as in a real animal.

Start with the tail end then as you progress your later stitches will overlap these earlier ones, again this is exactly how fur lies on a real animal. Abandon any thought of stitching along the outline - your fur should lie at an angle to the outline, giving you a slightly fluffy, rather than completely smooth mouse.

Start with the shadows making small straight stitches with the darkest colour. You don't have to complete the whole mouse in one colour before starting the next, it's easier to work in sections, going back to adjust if it doesn't look quite right.

Oh .. And please excuse the differing quality of the photos, I simply snapped as I stitched so the lighting changes all the time.

Now I've started to add some medium brown, concentrating it in the areas that will be most in shadow - around his bottom and back leg.

Continuing with the medium brown. Be sure to keep the stitches irregular and scattered - you don't want nice neat straight lines. If later stitches slightly overlap earlier ones, that's absolutely fine. The denser the stitching, the more lush and thick your mouse's fur will appear to be.

Realising my mistake with paws and tail I've now added them. I've also started to add the lightest shade of fur to his back - and also on his tummy which will be speckled and mainly cream.

Continuing in the same way, mixing the fur colours. You can see I've now added cream to his tummy.

I've added the shadow line beneath his tail and paws, and stitched his eye before I start work on his head. I've also gone back and added a few stitches to the base of his tail so the fur overlaps its end and you can see the speckled cream effect on his tummy.

Work continuing on his head. I've added claws in a single strand of dark brown floss and worked his pink ear in long and short stitch using the darker shade at the bottom of the ear and lighter at the top where the light would catch it. His cream fur continues under his chin and his nose is pink.

I have filled in the head with medium brown and light brown. Notice the stitches on the back ear run in a different direction to the fur on the head. His overall fur is still a little thin though, time to go back and fill in some of the gaps.

All finished! The tiny sparkle stitch in his eye really brings him to life! I have added his whiskers in a single strand of floss and added more stitching to his coat to fill in those gaps. A very handsome fellow indeed!

The other mice are worked in exactly the same way, though I haven't shown them stage by stage, here are larger photos so you can see their fur in detail:

Notice the cream fur around the top of his back leg - this helps delineate his leg line.

Again, cream and paler fur around the edge of his back leg. Darker fur along the right hand edge of his body.

I think mice are rather nice,
Their tails are long, their faces small
They haven't any chins at all!

They nibble things they shouldn't touch
And no one seems to like them much,
But I think mice are nice!

I think mice are rather nice,
Their tails are long, their faces small
They haven't any chins at all!
They ears are pink, their teeth are white,
They run about the house at night,
They nibble things they shouldn't touch,
And no one seems to like them much,
But I think mice are nice!

An Alphabet of Stitches (4)

LAZY DAISY STITCH
(Diagram 39)

Also named Daisy Stitch, Detached Chain Stitch, Link Stitch. For flower petals and leaves bring up the needle at the base of the traced shape, hold the thread down with the thumb of the left hand, take the needle through at the base, bring it out at the other end of the petal and pull it through over the held thread as shown in the diagram. Now take the needle through again making a tiny tying stitch over the end of the loop so that a stitch is formed as shown in the diagram. Bring the needle out at the base of the right hand petal

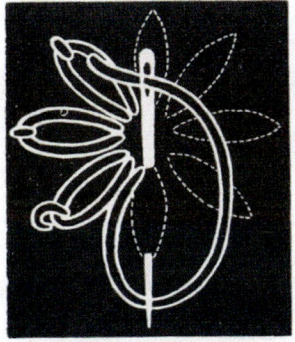 

Diagram 39   *Diagram 40*

Example of Long and Short Stitch.

ready for the next stitch. Work anti-clockwise round the flower head until it is complete. If the traced petal to be covered is a broad one work the lazy daisy stitch slightly open, that is, leave a slight space between the ends of the loop at the base. If necessary fill the centre of the loop with a small straight stitch, or if a more rounded shape is required fill with a french knot. Another variation is to work a small straight stitch of a second colour over the tying stitch.

LAZY DAISY STITCH—DOUBLE. *(Diagram 40)*

For large petals, etc., work two lazy daisies one enclosing the other as shown in diagram.

LEAF STITCH. *(Diagram 41)*

At the base of the shape to be worked bring the needle through at the left of the centre line. Insert the needle on the opposite margin a little higher than where it emerged and bring it through to the right of the centre and below the thread. Next insert the needle on the left margin and bring it through on the left side of the centre. Repeat these two movements, that is alternately right and left until the shape is covered with spaced stitches as shown. Leaves and borders are effectively embroidered in this stitch. Cover any traced outlines to the shapes which still show with Stem or Back Stitch, etc.

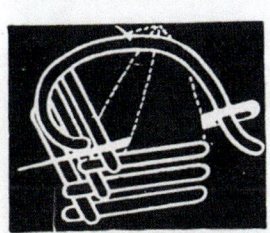

Diagram 41

LONG AND SHORT STITCH *(Diagrams 42 and 43)*

Also named Shading Stitch, Long and Short Stitch is mostly used for shaded effects but it can also be employed when large areas of one colour are required to be filled in and satin stitch is found to be impractical. An embroidery frame is necessary with this stitch to obtain satisfactory results. If worked in the hand puckering nearly always occurs. The first row of stitches should be alternately long and short, making a marked difference in length. Do not make any of the stitches too small. The direction of the stitches should follow the principles of natural growth, and can be indicated on the material with a pencil before work is begun. Stitches may be required to radiate or to lie quite evenly and parallel as shown in diagram 43. Diagram 42 shows the method of working. Begin at the

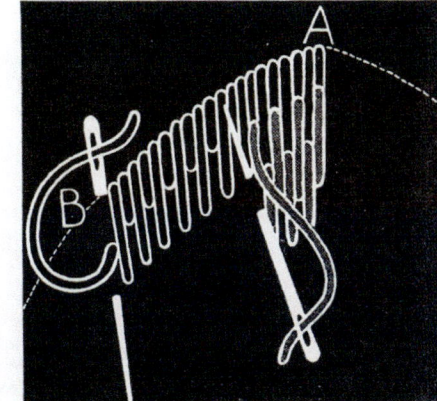

Diagram 42

tip of the object, i.e., at A in diagram, and work down to B; then complete the row by beginning again at A and working down the other side. Take the first row of stitches **down** on the outline. Now work the second row commencing at A as before, but this time the stitches are of **equal length, and set up and down** alternately to fit into the first row of stitches. On this row bring the needle up through the ends of the stitches of the first row so that they overlap. Many workers find it easier to again work down into the ends of the

Diagram 43

stitches on the previous row; this method is not incorrect. As many rows as are necessary are worked to fill up the form.

OUTLINE STITCH
(Diagram 44)

In Old English embroideries the stitch known by this name was Stem Stitch as worked in diagram 62, but in many modern embroideries the stitch shown here has come to be recognised as Outline. It is mainly used for pictures worked in monochrome effect called "needle etchings." A frame is necessary. Work from left to right. Bring the needle up a little way along the traced line. Insert it again a little distance behind this point and bring it up again the same distance in front (point A on diagram). Next take the needle through where the stitch before last emerged. Be sure to take the needle into the traced line every time and keep the stitches regular.

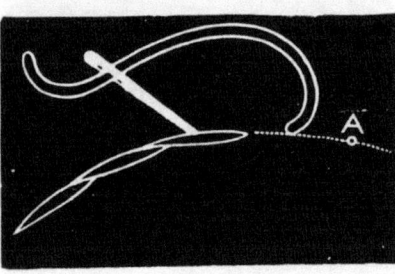

Diagram 44

OVERCAST EDGE
(Diagram 45)

The method shown here is used on small cut-out shapes to be seen in *Broderie Anglaise* and other forms of White Work. Straight and curved shapes are treated the same way.

Work around the outline of the shape with small Running Stitches. Knots must not be used, and a length of the thread should be left to be fastened in later. Cut across the shape in two directions within the Running Stitch outline. A circle is illustrated; in a square cut from corner to corner and in a leaf shape from point to point. Turn under one piece at a time and work over the folded edge and the running stitch in overcasting as shown. Press back the piece with the needle as you work, holding the work over the first finger of the left hand and working from left to right. In corners make a deeper stitch to emphasize them. Trim away surplus material from the back of the work and run in all ends. For small circular eyelets

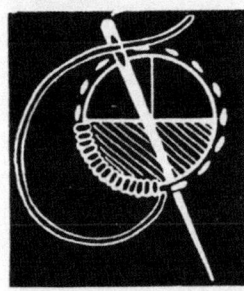

Diagram 45

Diagram 46

outline as before but instead of cutting the centre, pierce with a stiletto.

OVERCAST FILLING *(Diagram 46)*

Also named Russian Overcast Filling. An even fairly loosely woven fabric is required for this stitch. It is worked by the counted thread. First prepare the ground by cutting two threads and leaving two alternately in both directions to form a lattice. Overcast, Buttonhole or Hemstitch the cut edges of the shape; this is not shown in the diagram. Now overcast the lattice bars in a diagonal step direction; beginning at A make two stitches over the horizontal threads, one across the diagonal and two across the vertical threads up to B. Then commence at C and work the same way to D. Continue in this manner until all the lattice ground is covered.

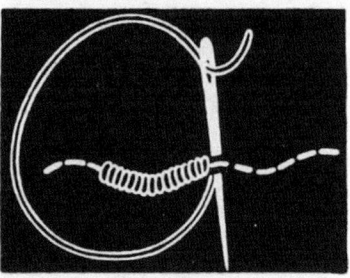

Diagram 47

OVERCAST OUTLINE STITCH *(Diagram 47)*

Work Running Stitch along the line to be covered. Then working from left to right take close straight stitches over this, picking up as little material with the needle as possible. This stitch is much used in White Work.

PEKINESE STITCH
(Diagram 48)

Work a row of Back Stitch, then in a contrasting colour for preference interlace this in the manner illustrated taking care not to pick up any of the ground fabric with the needle.

Diagram 48

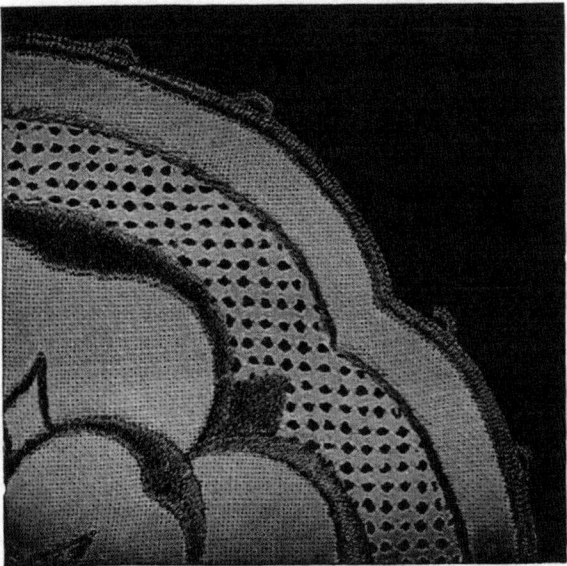

Example of Punch Work.

Page **Ten**

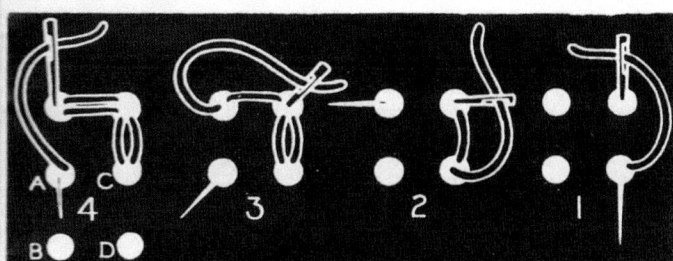

PUNCH STITCH.
(Diagram 49)

Diagram 49

This is what is termed a "Drawn Fabric" Stitch. It should be worked on a loosely woven ground by the counted thread but a simpler method and one less trying on the eyes is to use a transfer of equally spaced dots as a guide. The embroidery thread used should equal the thickness of a thread of the fabric. Work in rows from right to left. The method is shown in four separate stages numbering from right to left; note that *two* stitches are made over each side of the square and that only *three* sides are filled in on the first row. Stage 4 is really stage 1 repeated. Continue to the end of the row then turn the work in the hand and return along the next row closing the open side of the former row with one of the sides of the next row. This second row is worked as follows:—Having brought the needle out at A for the second time work BA, BA, BC, CA, CA, CD, CD, and so on to the end of the row.

RAISED ROSE STITCH
(Diagram 50)

Diagram 50

Also named Marie Rose Stitch. Small roses in garden pictures and floral designs can be worked with realistic effect in this stitch. Make a French Knot or two in the centre. Round this make three or four loose Stem Stitches, each one overlapping the previous stitch. Leave each stitch loose enough to make a loop. Work further rows of loops until the flower is complete. The outside row of all should be tighter than the others.

ROUMANIAN STITCH *(Diagram 51)*

Borders or leaf shapes can be filled with this stitch. Bring the needle through at the top left hand side, take it to the back on the opposite side and bring it through a short distance in towards the centre keeping the thread below the needle. Pull the stitch to tighten and make a long slanting stitch over it taking the needle to the back nearer the left side. These tying stitches must be kept even and exactly below each other.

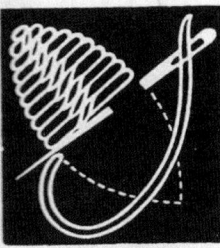

Diagram 51

Bring the needle out on the left margin again ready for the next stitch. Keep the stitches close together and do not leave spaces.

ROUMANIAN STITCH — VANDYKED. *(Diagram 52)*

This is a variation used chiefly for leaves as the centre tying stitch is worked quite straight (as in Fly Stitch) and forms a

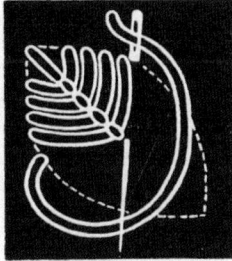

Diagram 52

neat vein effect. Begin as before but bring the needle through exactly in the centre of the shape and a little lower down instead of in line so that the stitch forms a V shape. The stitches can be worked closely or spaced.

RUNNING STITCH *(Diagram 53)*

Diagram 53

The diagram explains this very simple stitch. Make the stitches of equal lengths taking care to keep them in line and only picking up a thread or two of the ground fabric between.

RUNNING STITCH—WHIPPED
(Diagram 54)

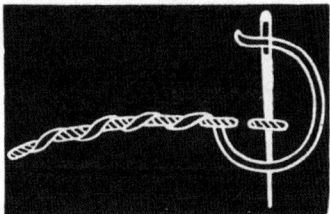

Diagram 54

Work a row of Running Stitch and then whip along this as illustrated taking care not to pick up any of the ground fabric with the needle; the eye of the needle can be passed through the stitches to avoid this.

SATIN STITCH. *(Diagrams 55 and 56)*

In order to avoid puckering an embroidery frame should be used for this stitch particularly if the design includes a fairly large amount of it. It is not the easiest of stitches and some practice will be required to get perfect results. Work straight stitches taking the needle

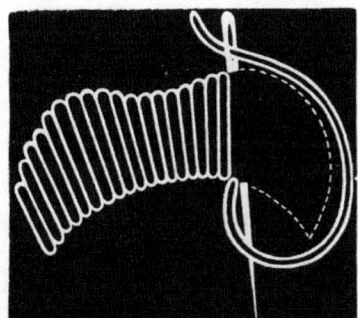

Diagram 55

Example of Satin Stitch.

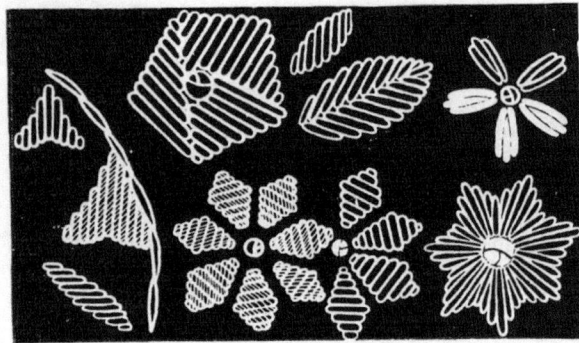

Diagram 56

through as illustrated in diagram 55. The stitches should lie fairly close together so that no background is visible but do not "crowd" them. Keep them even so that a flat surface is formed and preserve a neat firm edge to the shape being worked. Never make the stitches too long as this only gives the work a loose and untidy appearance. By varying the direction of the stitch on different portions of a design, an effect of light and shade can be given. The treatment of various floral shapes is shown in diagram 56. Satin stitch can also be worked by the counted thread on suitably woven fabrics. This method is used in Hardanger Embroideries.

Diagram 57

SATIN STITCH—PADDED
(Diagrams 57, 58)

In *Broderie Anglaise* and other forms of White Work, Satin Stitch is usually worked over a preliminary padding to give a more risen and firmer effect. Work Running Stitch just within the outline of the shape and then inside this work a few straight stitches in the opposite direction to that in which the Satin Stitch will be embroidered. Now proceed with the Satin Stitch. This method combined with overcast outline is used for embroidered initials.

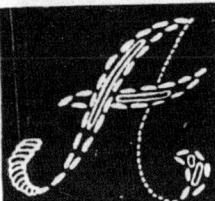

Diagram 58

SCROLL STITCH. *(Diagram 59)*

A decorative line stitch which could also be used for conventional water effects. Work from left to right. Bring the needle through at the end of the line to be worked.

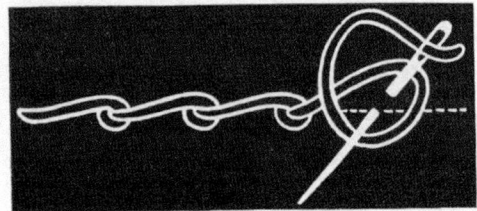

Diagram 59

With the working thread make a loop by carrying it first to the right and then to the left. Hold this down with the left thumb and insert the needle in the centre of it on the line as illustrated. Tighten the loop around the needle and pull through ready for the second stitch.

SPLIT STITCH
(Diagram 60)

Bring the needle up through the material and insert it a little in front of this point, now bring the needle up through the middle of this stitch, thus splitting it. If you find it difficult to bring the needle *up* through the thread reverse the process and split the previous stitch by taking the needle *down* through it. The only disadvantage with this last method is that the stitch is not so tidy on the back of the work. This stitch can be used for outlines and is also effective when worked in parallel rows for filling in drapery on figures, etc.; a frame will be required.

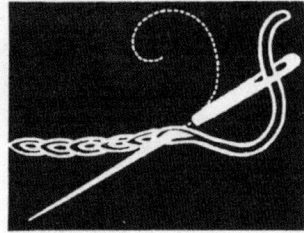

Diagram 60

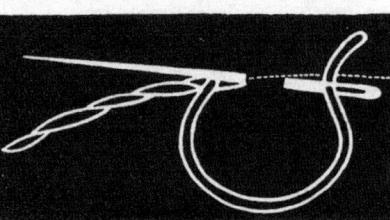

Diagram 61

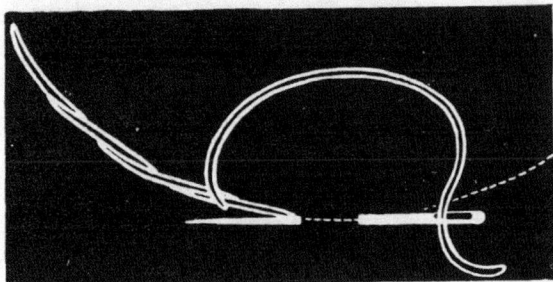

Diagram 62

Example of Stem Stitch

BUSTLE & SEW

The "Bustle & Sew Magazine" is a Bustle & Sew publication. To see my full range of Rosie & Bear publications, together with many more stitching, applique, softie and quilting projects please visit my website:

www.bustleandsew.com

Bustle & Sew designs

You can also find out about my Bustle & Sew Magazine on my website. This is my monthly e-zine packed with unique projects, articles, features and loads more, and is by far the best (and nicest!) way to build your collection of Bustle & Sew patterns…

You'll never be stuck for ideas again!! Just visit the magazine page on my website to learn more:

www.bustleandsew.com/magazine.

Printed in Great Britain
by Amazon.co.uk, Ltd.,
Marston Gate.

A Bustle & Sew Publication

Copyright © Bustle & Sew Limited 2012

The right of Helen Dickson to be identified as the author of this work has been asserted in accordance with the Copyright, Designs and Patents Act 1988.

All rights reserved. No part of this publication may be reproduced, stored in a retrieval system or transmitted in any form, or by any means, without the prior written permission of the author, nor be otherwise circulated in any form of binding or cover other than that in which it is published and without a similar condition being imposed on the subsequent purchaser.

Every effort has been made to ensure that all the information in this book is accurate. However, due to differing conditions, tools and individual skills, the publisher cannot be responsible for any injuries, losses and other damages that may result from the use of the information in this book.

ISBN-13: 978-1484106082

ISBN-10: 1484106083

First published 2013 by:
Bustle & Sew
Coombe Leigh
Chillington
Kingsbridge
Devon TQ7 2LE
UK

www.bustleandsew.com